Inheritance

To Hubert —
With high regard for all
your achievements —
And with all best wishes —

[signature]

13/8/21

d McDonald
s in St. Kitts, W.I.
a Camilla Seheult at
ch, Trinidad July 9th 1932.
ltural Dept, Trinidad 1923-1929
ch Chemist + Lecturer in physics +
I.C.T.A of Trinidad 1930-1936
torney, Gordon Grant + Co. Ltd. 1936-1966
- 1966. Moved to Cliff House Hodge Bay
May 1st, 1973. Died Aug. 6th, 1995 at
Cliff House, Antigua

West Indies

|
Son of Hilda M. Edwards
M. McDonald + Hilda M. Edwards
Practioner Leeward Islands, Antigua +
t. Kitts, Nevis. Born April 16, 1870.
d Hilda Ellen Maud Edwards Aug. 26 1902
Mary's Collegiate Chapel, Port Elizabeth,
Africa (Service with R.A.M.C. in Boer War).
ice Medical Research on Ancylostomiasis
k Worm) and Malaria in Antigua.
(Reports in British Medical Journal)
Died Cliff House, Hodges Bay Antigua
1951

|
Son of
John Scotland McDonald
(see page 2)

Inheritance

The Story of
a West Indian Family

By Ian McDonald
Edited and Illustrated by
Robin McDonald

Copyright © Ian McDonald 2020

All rights reserved. Except for use in reviews, no part of this publication may be reproduced or transmitted in any form or by any means, electronic or mechanical, including photocopy, recording, or any information storage or retrieval system, without permission in writing from the publishers.

ISBN: 978-976-8244-43-7

Design & Layout by Paria Publishing Co. Ltd.

Printing by Lightningsource.com

Contents

Other Books by Ian McDonald	VI
Author's Note	VII
Acknowledgements	VIII
Dedication	IX
Preface	1
William Spry	5
Judith Baynes	10
Seheults and De Verteuils	12
Edward Dacres Baynes	16
Edwin Donald Baynes	21
Thomas Goodall	24
The Edwards Family	27
Samuel McDonald	31
Ian Donald Roy McDonald	33
Dr. William Maclachlan McDonald	36
Leo Seheult	40
Donald McDonald	43
Hilda McDonald	46
Clydie McDonald and his wife Gyppie	51
Emily Seheult née Gray	54
Uncle Bertie Harragin	56
Sir Arthur William Baynes McDonald	59
Archie McDonald And Thelma Seheult	62
Afterthought	67
Family Trees	70

Other Books by Ian McDonald

FICTION
The Hummingbird Tree (1969)

POETRY
Mercy Ward (1988)
Essequibo (1992)
Jaffo The Calypsonian (1994)
Between Silence And Silence (2003)
The Comfort Of All Things (2012)
River Dancer (2016)
New And Collected Poems (2018)
People Of Guyana (with Peter Jailail) (2018)
Poems For Mary (2020)

DRAMA
Tramping Man (1969)

NON FICTION
Cloud of Witnesses (2012)
A Love Of Poetry (2013)
An Abounding Joy – Essays on sport compiled edited and annotated by Clem Seecharan (2019)

EDITED
Selected Poems of Martin Carter (1989)
Collected Poems of A.J. Seymour (with J. de Weever) (2000)

ANTHOLOGY (with Stewart Brown)
The Bowling Was Super Fine – West Indian Cricket Writing (2012)

Author's Note

Born in 1933 in St. Augustine, Trinidad, son of Archie and Thelma McDonald nee Seheult. Educated at Queen's Royal College in Port of Spain and Cambridge University where he took an Honours Degree in History. Lived and worked since 1955 in Guyana where he became Director of Marketing and Administration in the Guyana Sugar Industry and CEO of the Sugar Association of the Caribbean. Played at Wimbledon in the 1950s and captained Cambridge and then Guyana at lawn tennis and subsequently the West Indies Davis Cup Team in the 1960s. Author of the Hummingbird Tree and 8 books of poetry and won the Guyana prize for Literature in 1992, 2002 and 2012. Editorial Assistant to the Sridath Ramphal West Indian Commission in 1991/92. Member of the P.J. Patterson Committee on the Governance of West Indian Cricket in 2007/08. Chairman of the Stabroek News and has written a weekly column for that newspaper for 30 years. Awarded Guyana's Golden Arrow of Achievement 1986. Honorary Doctorate of Letters from UWI, St. Augustine in 1997. Fellow of the Royal Society of Literature since 1970. Married to Mary Callender with sons Jamie and Darren and a son Keith from a previous marriage. "Antiguan by ancestry, Trinidadian by birth, Guyanese by adoption, West Indian by conviction"

Acknowledgements

I must above all thank my parents for preserving the abundant documents, records, letters and photographs which has enabled me to summon this narrative from the shadows.

I thank Mark Seheult, cousin and keeper of the Seheult family records, for providing the documented history of my mother's forbears.

I am also most grateful to Susan Lowes, Director Research and Evaluation, Teachers College, Columbia University, and Judy Forward, who have both provided important information.

I acknowledge with thanks the work of William Eliot, from whose privately printed - A Short Biography of Edward Dacres Baynes I have derived information for this narrative.

I thank and praise Alice Besson, and her staff at Paria Publishing, for the care and creativity which has gone into this book. How good they are at their job!

And this book would not have come to fruition without the help of my sister Robin in editing and providing illustrations. She encouraged me every step of the way.

To
My Sisters and Brother
Heather, Gillian, Robin, Monica and Archie
With thanks and love.

ANTIGUA. W.I.

Arthur Elliot Edwards (known as the young doctor) married
- Jan 12th, 1853 in Antigua
Medical Practitioner.
April 17th, 1897 in Antigua
Son of

Henry Edwards, Seaton, England
1st 1809 at Frogmore
Antigua July 1842
Died in Antigua 1842 - 1899
Saints, Antigua

Hilda
Born
Married
on Aug.
Christ Ch
Died June
Berks, Engla
(Antigua as
St. Johns, Men
British commi
World War II sh
in charge of Rad
and correspondent
Her poems were p
& "Stardust" by the
daughter

Preface

It goes without saying. Any person who ever lived – for a hundred years or just a sad flash of time – is connected to a host of ancestors.

Every one of their stories is wondrous and unusual if told looking back. Even those who barely blinked in the marvelous light of life had an intricacy of forebears varied and strange as long chronicled royalty. Two daughters were born to me, Michelle lived one week, Paulette a few hours. Sweet mayflies. They are part of this story too.

There I am – a twig on the McDonald family tree amidst the larger forest of connected families. One day perhaps I will write down what I remember of my own life. But my purpose now is to recall briefly something of the family I was born into, a few of their stories, achievements, tragedies, stumbles if I notice them and can bear to tell because stumbles can be most interesting of all – the dramas and lessons which caught in my mind.

How could any such account be anything other than selective in the extreme? Unless I was Proust – and I know in my heart that every family deserves a Proust – but then even his seven-volume Remembrance of Things Past included only a selection of his memories of family and friends. There are those whom

I would like to write books about and if I was scholarly enough there might be enough in the record. There are scores of others who deserve at least a passing, loving reference but will not get even that because in the time I have for composition they do not come to mind or are left out lest the canvas become too crowded with the sketches.

The huge majority of our ancestors, having emerged from eternity, when they die quickly vanish again into endless time. Some gleam in the light of human history briefly and then they disappear. A very few, perhaps rescued by scholars for a time, glow in fame a while longer. And just one or two, in a small corner of the communal memory, may be remembered for a hundred years or more. There they all throng in the crowded family trees immediate and extended (see family trees at the end of the book). Let me call a few out of the shadows. Famous in their time or obscure, they have lodged in my mind, come alive in my imagination. Peripheral – or all-important, as in the case of my parents – they gave me substance in the womb.

I write about them without looking too closely at the reference material. Memories that matter are not always based on facts when checked or on events and people that are momentously recorded. But such memories can have great power and beauty creating myths more transfiguring than factual truth. The unremarkable and unnoticed take on a Kubla Khan intensity. If not why do I now recall great-aunt Anna? She was my mother's aunt, an ordinary spinster who lived to 92 and did nothing famous though she was known in her time for the beautiful clothes she sewed. But she loved me and I loved her. She is part of the finely ground dust of history except for a memory like this. When I was a schoolboy I stayed at 84 Dundonald Street in Port-of-Spain to attend Queens Royal College during the week, going home to St. Augustine at the weekends. My grandmother, Aunt Muriel and great-aunt Anna lived at 84 Dundonald Street and they were all good to me beyond measuring. Many nights I sat with great-aunt Anna and she told me stories of the old days and when I was sitting exams or had to

84 Dundonald Street, POS, Trinidad - Home of Anna Collins, Muriel Evans née Gray, and Emily Seheult née Gray after her husband Leo Seheult died in 1939- the three lived there until the death of both Emily Seheult and Muriel Evans in January 1956.. Great Aunt Anna Collins moved into a home for the elderly. Photo taken in 1999 – house is presently owned by the Trinidad Govt.

---

play in tennis tournaments she said her rosary for my success. She described the blazing blood-red sunsets which lasted for months after the Mount Pelee volcano eruption. I have never forgotten the fiery sunsets she described and the dances she attended when she was a girl and the old-time carnivals she loved to remember. And I have never forgotten the rosaries she told so confidently for me to do well. She is part of what I inherited. So she lives a while. Through me there are those who see her still, rocking in her chair, saying her rosary for a schoolboy. It is over 70 years. The sound of her chair as she rocked entered my remembrance for good. There was a distinctive, extended crack at the end of each rock – creakkk, creak, creakkk, creak. No sound exactly like it since the universe began.

One night recently, at the age of 85, I woke from a dream as a lovely dawn began to break over my wife Mary's garden. I had been in a house of many rooms. In all the rooms there was the sound of animated creakkk, creak, creakkk, creak of a rocking chair distinct above the laughter. I knew it at once as I woke. I recognized it deep down in wherever I am in me. Great-Aunt Anna was saying her rosary for me, for all of us. Everything would be all right.

William Spry

One ancestor loomed large when I was a little boy. At Redcliff House in Redcliff Street, the McDonald house in St. John's, Antigua, I visited with my parents it must have been in the late 1930s, early 1940s.

There someone — was it my father but I more think it was my grandmother or grandfather McDonald — told me the story of a family hero who had fought in the sea battle, the Battle of the Saints, for the British against the French. I looked it up. Indeed, my great great great great grandfather, Lieutenant William Spry, had been on board HMS Formidable which had done gallant service when Admiral Rodney won the great naval battle against the French in 1782 near Dominica. The story I was told captured William Spry's heroics in details marvelous for a boy — the smoke-shrouded deck, the furious discharge of guns, the shouts of triumph and the cries of agony, even I seem to remember hand-to-hand encounters, cut and counter-cut, with deadly, flashing cutlasses. All made up for a little boy, I'm sure. Except one detail I wonder about: "Across his back a burning rope fell and branded him — a mark of honour about which he boasted all his life." Perhaps it was so indeed. I even see the rigging fall in flames.

> *Dearest Mania's Brothers Letters.*
>
> *Emma Spry Sampson*
> *I hope my grandchildren will value these letters —*
> *My Uncle William Spry my Mother's brother was killed when we, England conquered Bermuda*
> *West Indies*
>
> *There is a tablet erected to the memory of my uncle William Spry at Bermuda West Indies. Emma Spry Sampson. Tablet in Cathedral or Church*

Note from William Spry's niece indicating her where her uncle was killed.

Hulett's South African Refineries, Limited.

DIRECTORS:
W. S. R. EDWARDS, CHAIRMAN.
A. S. L. HULETT, J.P.
~~~~~~~~~~~
WM. A. CAMPBELL, J.P.
W. FITZGERALD.

CECIL PLATT.
W. B. CALDER.
G. J. CROOKES.
R. S. ARMSTRONG.
G. H. HULETT.

P.O. BOX 1501.
TELEGRAMS: "HULSAR," DURBAN.
TELEPHONE: 2-5171.

STABILITY BUILDINGS.
310 SMITH STREET.
DURBAN.

11th January, 1940.

Dearest Hilda,

With reference to the copies of the letters from Spry that I enclose, you will notice that there one or two blanks. This was where the paper perished in the fold, but I have now had the letters treated with a preparation by an Archivist, and have had them framed, so they are practically indestructible now.

Your

Mrs. Hilda McDonald,
St. Johns,
ANTIGUA....B.W.I.

Letter from Reggie Edwards, Hilda McDonald's brother, dated 11th Jan. 1940 attaching letter from William Spry

---

AGC/14/8
(8)

SPRY, Midshipman William   fl. 1782.

Holograph, to his Parents.
Dated from the Formidable, at Sea. April 14th, 1782.

With description of the Battle of the Saints.

37 MS. 1653.

Letter from MIDSHIPMAN WILLIAM SPRY to his parents, dated from the "Formidable" at sea, 14th April 1782, with eye-witness account of the Battle of the Saints.

No 10
                    Formidable at Sea Aprill 14th 1782

Honrd Father & Mother)

                At our Arrival in the West Indies
which was February 14th we were inform'd
that the Island of St Kitts was taken by the
French and that they were in the greatest
Shiets Immaginable, we have had nothing
happen'd since our Arrival worth Relating
till Aprill the 7th when Capt Byron of the
Andromache brought in Intelligence (to St Lucie
which place we where then at) that the
Count de Grasse the French Admrl had put to Sea
from Martinico with 32 Sail of the Line and
it was Suppos'd he Intended to make an attack
on the Island of Jamaica, the Instant St George
heard it he swore on the Quarter deck that he
would put Jamaica out of their heads and
we Immediately put to Sea with 35 Sail of
the Line in pursuit of them, on the 9th at
day light we got sight of them close under
the Island of Dominico and at 10 OClock 20.
of our Ships came to an Action with them
the Formidable was one of the 21. we fought
them 42 Minutes when they made off being to
Windward of us in this Action we had 3 Men
kill'd & 7 Wounded one of our Lieuts was killed
we kept sight of them till the 12th when we
had a most bloody Action which lasted from
7 OClock in the morning till a after 6 at Night
however we knock'd all their fleet to Atoms

Letter from William Spry to his parents dated April 14th, 1782

almost and we can boldly venture to say t'was the best day that old England ever Saw, but I'll not keep you in Suspense by writing a long Epistle but will give you an account of the French Ships we have taken & Destroy'd —

	Guns	Men	Additional Troops	
La Ville de Paris	112	1500	200	taken
La Glorieux	74	900	100	taken
La Hector	74	900	100	taken
L'Ardent	64	700	100	taken
La Cæsar	74	900	100	burnt
La Zodiac	74	900	100	Sunk

She struck to the Formidable after having 175 Men Kill'd and 100 Wounded, the Count de Grasse was onboard this Ship, she is the finest that ever sail'd from any Port whatever, is much larger than the Formidable and has upwards of a Million of Money Onboard —

between the Formidable & Namur, it was most horrible to see this Ship when she came to us she was all to pieces then the Namur & us fir'd a Broadside each into her & she sunk Immediately — I have nothing more worth Relating so pray be so kind as to give my Compliments to all Friends Love to Brother & Sister and accept of my most humble duty to Yourselves, from

P:S: Pray do be so kind as to give Mr Hendersons Comp:ts to Mr Brown the Sail Seller & tell them he is slightly Wounded as is Mr Martin —

Your most Dutifull Son
Wm Spry

NB: in this last action we had 7 Kill'd & 13 Wounded

Judith Baynes

My long life has been filled with interest and marvels in the main. When I hear about a young person who dies by accident or sudden, unforgiving illness I think of the times of love and beauty and infinite experiences he or she never had the chance of knowing. They missed awaking to ten thousand dawns of wonder.

My five times great grandmother, Judith Baynes, born in 1736, was married to Surgeon Major Arthur Baynes.

An illustration of the fireworks display celebrating the Dauphin's marriage to Marie-Antoinette, May 30th, 1770 (Bibliothèque nationale de France)

They were living in Gibraltar when Judith's father, Sir John Lambert, a banker resident in Paris at the time of the marriage of the Dauphin of France (later King Louis XVI) to the Austrian princess Marie Antoinette, invited Judith to the festivities accompanying the great royal event. It was the greatest public event of its time. What a thrill to be invited! Imagine the excitement, the unprecedented glamour in prospect, the setting out for the social adventure of a lifetime.

In one of those strokes of fate which families in every generation encounter, on May 30th, 1770, the marvelous fireworks display Judith was bidden to attend in all her finery went tremendously, tragically amiss. Judith Baynes, aged 34, mother of five, was one of those killed in the terrible, famous accident. In those days it took some time for the news to get to Gibraltar. For some reason I think a lot about that point.

Seheults and De Verteuils

L ate in life I am fascinated to discover that my great great grandfather, Jean Jacques Alexandre Seheult, was born in Nantes into the heart of the French Revolution.

When I was a boy in St. Augustine books about the exciting times of the French Revolution – generally featuring heroic deeds performed against the dastardly Revolutionaries by such marvelous characters as the Scarlet Pimpernel – were among my favourites. Later I read with reverence for his style and philosophy Edmund Burke's eloquent anti-Revolution polemic Reflections on the French Revolution. And then at Cambridge, studying history, as one of the special subjects in my final year I chose the Diplomatic History of the French Revolution from a British point of view. Most of this reading, which I remember enjoying so much, tended to paint the Revolution in dangerous, even villainous,

Jean Jacques Alexandre Seheult
Image courtesy Mark Seheult

light. But I found – quite honestly to my late delight – that my great great grandfather was born into the belly of the beast.

Jean Jacques Seheult was born in Nantes on 14th April, 1794 (le vingt cinq germinal au deux de la republique). His father Alexandre Nicholas Seheult was supplies clerk to the Revolutionary Armee de l'Ouest. At that time Nantes was a notoriously Revolutionary town. The year previous to Jean Jacques' birthday the National Convention in Paris, suspecting that there were royalists at large in Nantes, sent its representative to "cleanse" the area. In order to speed up the "cleansing" the representative ordered prisoners to be crammed onto barges and the barges were then scuttled in the middle of the Loire river – an atrocity which has remained infamous as the noyades de Nantes (Nantes Drownings). To be fair to the Revolution, the National Convention rapidly summoned the representative back to Paris and cut off his head!

In the confusion of those Revolutionary, and then Napoleonic, years little is known of the boyhood and youthful career of Jean Jacques (except that for 9 years he was a ships broker). However, he must have been shrewd and conscientious in whatever he did since by 1820 he was prospering as a businessman and trader. One thing we do know is that he was one of the first traders to ship goods from Nantes to Trinidad. And something in the business, or in what he heard, led to a great decision. The exact date of his arrival in Trinidad we do not know but it was probably sometime in the period 1820-24. Thereafter he quickly established himself, did well in business and settled in the Arima area among other French families.

He made the transition often chosen by ambitious and successful traders: he set about acquiring agricultural property and becoming a plantation owner. Records show that by 1830, when he was 36, Jean Jacques owned a goodly estate, Santa Rosa, just south of Arima. He also aspired to official recognition in British Trinidad. In 1829 he applied to be Colonial Agent for

France in Trinidad. For many years his application was declined but he persevered and, finally, in 1839, Jean Jacques became the first French Vice Consul in Trinidad in which position he served until his death in 1865. For his contribution to commercial relations between France and the English Antilles he was awarded the honour "Chevalier L' Ordre Imperial de la Legion d'Honneur".

Where to me the story becomes particularly fascinating is in the marriage of Jean Jacques. In 1837, when he was 43, he married my great great grandmother Anne Josephe Cecilia Losea de Verteuil, aged 28, of ancient and noble lineage and very much of the Royalist persuasion – as opposed to Jean Jacques' Revolutionary roots. The de Verteuils were indeed an ancient and noble family. As early as 1080 we learn of a Denis de Verteuil who made a donation to the famous Abby of Maillezais in the Vendee. By the 14th century the de Verteuils were rich merchants owning a large part of the town of Bordeaux. We then learn that "their military reputation was made in the wars of the 17th, 18th and 19th centuries and as frequently happens as their valour increased their wealth correspondingly declined."

Royalist through and through for sure. At about the time of Jean Jacques' Seheult birth in 1794 the two families may indeed have been very closely opposed. Jean Jacques' father was with the Revolutionary Army of the West – while Cecilia Losea's father, Sir Michel Julien de Verteuil (Knighted by Queen Victoria and the Pope) was fighting with the L'larmee Royal De Vendee in Belgium and later with the Dutch against the Revolutionaries. The fathers of the bride and groom may not exactly have drawn sabers against each other but not far off.

I like to think about it. Life is such a rigmarole. Such different histories melded into one new adventure. I wonder if Jean Jacques and his bride Cecilia Losea knew any of the details and, if they did, how they talked of their parents and grandparents? The mixing of blood indeed.

What they could not foresee, of course, I know – not only the ironic connecting of Revolutionary and Royal but, of all things, the future mixing of the blood of those ancient enemies France and Britain. I know because I am.

Edward Dacres Baynes

An English warrior was my great great great grandfather Edward Dacres Baynes – but much more than a warrior: a considerable poet and a custodian of empire of high rank. I think he must have been at least semi-famous in his day. Certainly he and his family were surprising and dramatic. His brother fought at Waterloo and was wounded in that great and pivotal battle. When I grew up and got to know about this distant relative I hoped he was wounded helping to repulse the last mighty and despairing charge of Napoleon's Imperial Guard – and why should I not claim that he was?

Edward Dacres Baynes himself was clearly a dashing soldier. Post-Napoleon, stationed at his outpost in Malta, he was on a walking holiday in Italy with a friend when they came to a Convent where they sought refreshment. I like to imagine what might then have happened. But, whatever did, it ended with a novice nun running off with him – my great great great grandmother Francesca Agatha Di San Giuliano, the daughter of an Italian Nobleman the Marchese Di San Giuliano. How I would love to know every detail of their romance and elopement!

Post-soldiering, Edward Dacres pursued a career in the Colonial Service. He, wife and growing family found themselves in the West Indies – first in Jamaica where he was a stipendiary magistrate protecting the interest of ex-slaves, then in Montserrat when he became a contentious President of the Council and

My uncle Arthur William Baynes McDonald standing next to the memorial

Arthur Baynes
A high Official in Military and Civil Affairs, and by several gifts performed — the two islands already held — high esteem. To the grief of his friends and in the fulness of Honours he died in middle life, matched by envious death in his thirty-eighth year. He was a fearless man and free, contemptuous of fate. He was no slave, but the cultivator and protector of Justice.

finally in Antigua where he settled and retired and where death found him on 5th November, 1863.

His career in the islands was full of confrontation and controversy. In Jamaica he fought for the rights of ex-slaves against the planters and their allies. There he founded a newspaper **The West Indian** "to spread useful knowledge and to show that distinctions of race were not fundamental to human society....." In Jamaica also he endured what must have been a devastating, emotional outrage in the case he brought – but did not win – against an English Army officer for abducting and raping his daughter. When he was President in Montserrat he was accused of mishandling funds contributed by the public to hurricane relief and spent a good part of the rest of his official life in voluminous efforts to clear his name and establish what was due to him.

But long before all that he was a poet. A considerable poet, at least in output. Here is a list of his publications:

Ovid's Epistles, Translations, Volume I. (1818). He translated seven Epistles, intending to translate fourteen other Epistles in Volume II but there is no evidence these were ever published, if indeed they were translated.

Love and Laudanum, or, The Sleeping Dose: A Farce in Two Acts. (1818).

Childe Harold in the Shades. An Infernal Romaunt. (1819).

Pastorals. Ruggiero. With Other Poems. (1819).

Annals of England, A Poem, in Four Books. (Published in 1847 but likely written in the 1820s).

I have looked and he certainly didn't get rave reviews. And he is not at all likely to be discovered as an unpolished jewel in another age. But I take pride in noting that his writings have not completely disappeared as so much writing – and indeed so much else – does and will.

After 200 years the poetry he wrote still lives. There are for all to find Amazon links to Scholars Choice Editions (no less) of both his **Annals of England** and his **Translations of Ovid's Epistles**. I ordered these beautiful editions for myself and as I handle them I am pleased to salute my extraordinary and passionate ancestor.

Here for at least a taste of his verse are his stanzas **XLIV** and **XLV** of **Childe Harold in the Shades**. They give quite a vivid pen picture of that great English Doctor of Letters Sam Johnson:

XLIV

"Unmanner'd, self-will'd, stubborn, stern, austere
Pedantic, solemn, prejudic'd and proud;
In knowledge a deep fount, profound, yet clear;
In wit the flame which cleaves the summer cloud;
In argument a torrent fierce and loud,
O'erbearing opposition; a philosopher,
Yet credulous as childhood, though endow'd
with might from error's face the mask to tear:
An elephant when wrath, when pleas'd a dancing bear.

XLV

Of kind affections, but in act uncouth;
Not brooking contradiction in the fray
Of tongues, and seeking victory more than truth;
Blind to his own defects, life's transient day,
Like mastiff o'er his bone, he growl'd away;
Too apt to wield a club, he often smote
Some teasing fly which buzz'd around in play;
And such too oft his style (himself I quote),
A tea-pot in a storm, sound signifying nought."

Edward Dacres Baynes was clearly driven hard by high emotion. I get the impression that he must have lived on a knife's edge of drama a great deal of his life, that his strongly beating heart was in the right place, that his love and loyalty and ambition for family was supreme, that his instinct for what is right was absolutely secure. He seems to have given up writing poetry quite early. But who knows what poems he passionately acted out in the rest of his life. As I write this brief remembrance, I think of the magnificent words he spoke about the results of an election to the Council of Montserrat in 1858, two years before the Civil War in America began and Lincoln set out to save the Union and free the slaves.

> *"I see with much gratification, in the result of the late general election, an irrefragable proof of equality, not only by right, but of actual participation in power on the part of that class who for so many years were denied the possession of all political privileges. The present Assembly is composed of six white and the same number of coloured gentlemen, an unerring sign that the age of prejudice has passed away, and that the day is near at hand when all distinction of colour between members of the human family will cease to exist; black and white will be no more remarked in our political and social relations than in the accidental differences of complexion between Europeans at the present day – a day when it shall be fully recognized that Virtue, Talent and Education only should open the path of public honours and private respectability."*

I note with a certain pride that his sentiment is echoed in a rather better known oration 105 years later delivered on the steps of the Lincoln Memorial in Washington.

Edwin Donald Baynes

One of Edward Dacres Baynes's sons was Edwin Donald, my great great grandfather. He had a distinguished career and was Colonial Secretary of the Leeward Islands in the period.

All my life I have been a strong believer in West Indian unity and was distressed when the Federation of the West Indies failed in 1962. I was Editorial Assistant to Sir Shridath Ramphal's West Indian Commission and helped draft its Report **Time For Action** which fervently advocated a closer union of West Indian states. At the end of my own career I became CEO of the Sugar Association of the Caribbean which brought together all the West Indian states' sugar industries.

It therefore fascinates me to read this account of my great great grandfather's tenure as Colonial Secretary:

"The major political issue of Edwin's period as Colonial Secretary, first in Montserrat and then in Antigua, was the Federation of the Leeward Islands. The idea was first canvassed by the British Treasury in April 1860, when sanctioning a loan for Dominica. The Treasury reasoned that Federation would provide much needed economies in the civil and judicial establishments. In 1867 a proposal to create a Federation of the Windward and Leeward Islands, with the Governor of Barbados as Governor-in-Chief, had

stirred up great opposition in Barbados and the Windwards. In the following year, Sir Benjamin Pine, the Governor of the Leeward Islands, explored the possibility of federating the Leeward Islands only. In a paper preserved in the Colonial Office records, he set out the arguments, for and against:
Pro:
1. *Federation would restore the ancient connection of the islands.*
2. *A common commercial connection would draw them closer.*
3. *It was expedient to have a uniform legal system within the islands.*
4. *With a wider field, the caliber of Assembly men elected would improve.*
5. *Public issues would be removed from influence of local cliques.*
6. *There would be an economy of scale in all administration.*
7. *There were a number of specific issues that ought to be treated in a uniform manner throughout the islands: Post and Telegraphs; Currency; Weights and Measures; Copyrights and Patents; Quarantine; Education; Immigration; Lunatic asylums, Prisons; Police and Militia, Property Law; Insolvency Procedures; Transfer of Civil Personnel; Audit and Public Accounts.*

Con:
1. *Local opposition, based on the fear of richer islands having to support poorer ones.*
2. *In St. Kitts, Thomas Hardtman, a leading planter and estate owner, had taken a leading part in obtaining signatures to a Memorial opposing Federation.*
3. *Nevis objected to the "unconstitutional and arbitrary conduct" of Pine in forcing Federation on the islands against the wishes of the Colonialists, their independence "won by self denial and painful privations."*

The more things change, the more they remain the same.

Edwin Donald Baynes who lived an active, hard-working and productive but relatively normal life as far as the record shows, leads me back awhile to an earlier and more flamboyant branch of the family the details of which I have only lately discovered in this age when so much is more discoverable than ever before.

Thomas Goodall

Edwin Donald Baynes married Sarah Goodall. She was therefore thrice great grandmother to myself and siblings.

And that link certainly brings a further and varied fascination to our far-flung West Indian story. For Sarah Goodall's grandfather was Thomas Goodall and her grandmother was Charlotte Goodall (née Stanton) and they for sure had interesting tales to tell their grandchildren. Certainly in their life-times this couple must have made the headlines, however, headlines were made two centuries ago.

At 13 Thomas ran away to sea from a perfectly respectable family and therefore followed a career of extreme adventure and danger which saw him in naval action against Britain's enemies whoever they might be, commander eventually of privateers, the capturer of rich prizes on the seas' highways and a stint as adviser to Henri Christophe in Haiti which evidently entitled him to be known as "Admiral of Hayti" in his official portrait.

Early in his swashbuckling career Thomas Goodall saw a young actress at a theatre and subsequently, in 1787, married Charlotte Stanton who was becoming known as an up and coming actress and later became celebrated for her Shakespearian and other roles in "breeches parts," playing to considerable acclaim such cross-dressing roles as Viola in "Twelfth Night" and, especially, Adeline in George Coleman's popular "The Battle of Hexham."

They must have been a noteworthy couple in their contrasting vivid and extraordinary careers. So the fame or notoriety can be imagined when Thomas Goodall in 1813 fought an action "for criminal conversation" against William Fletcher, an attorney

Thomas Goodall   Charlotte Goodall
                                  née Stenton

who for long while Thomas had been abroad, had been his representative in London for robbing him for years and, moreover, even more sensationally, acquiring Thomas's wife Charlotte as his mistress. I think I can imagine the sensation – and, I would have thought, the family confusion since by then Thomas and Charlotte had produced – somehow finding the time – eight children. Be that as it may, Thomas won his action and was awarded the considerable sum at the time of £5,000. After which, as far as can be ascertained, the couple resumed their married life on a reasonably even keel.

I wonder, though, what Edwin Donald Baynes, as he administered the affairs of the Leeward Islands, must have thought of his grand-in-laws and their dramatic and colourful lives. And yet, why would he have been in the slightest astounded? After all, his own father had not lived an exactly unperturbed life. Come to think of it, whoever does?

The Edwards Family

The Edwards family was one of Antigua's grand families. My grandmother, Hilda McDonald née Edwards was grand daughter of William Henry Edwards, the Old Doctor of island fame. In the telling of it in my presence, the Old Doctor, as he was always called, was a dominating figure in the life of the family and in the life of the island. He must have been a memorable character.

I reproduce here the obituary which appeared in the Antigua newspaper at the time of his death which captures some of the flourishes of a man and physician whose impact on the community was long remembered.

"Dr. William Henry Edwards: (The Old Doctor) obituary notice in Antigua Daily paper: June 1899

The late Dr. Wm. H. Edwards - at 6:55 on Sunday evening the 4th June, William Henry Edwards answered his last "call" readily and cheerfully as was his want throughout his long career.

Dr. Edwards had been in failing health for some months and had repeated warning of the approach of the inevitable; but no warning, no advice could lessen the vitality that seemed to defy age, disease and death: during the last week his activity appeared almost unnatural; it seemed as though he were trying to get all that he could out of the few days left to him.

On Saturday, he attended a meeting at the Agricultural Society's Room, and in the afternoon went to a reception at the Chief Justice's Residence. That evening he complained of headache, but went to bed at his usual hour apparently well. About 1 o'clock Mrs. Edwards heard someone groaning and on going into the Doctor's room found him on the floor apparently paralyzed. He remained unconscious for a few hours, but he knew his hour had come. He became unconscious not long after receiving the last sacrament at the hands of the Rev. H.Y. Shepherd and passed quietly away in the evening. He died as he wished and almost expected. The almost unnatural calmness of his death was a striking contrast to the ceaseless turmoil of his life. No man enjoyed life more. No man feared death less.

Dr. Edwards - "The 'Old' Doctor" of everybody was born in Devonshire on August 1st, 1817 and arrived in Antigua in July 1842, beginning his long professional career as assistant to Dr. Odlum at English Harbour: In 1844 he started practice on his own account and was at once eminently successful. For nearly half a century his practice extended over the length and breadth of Antigua.

On Aug. 1st, 1844, he married Miss Ledeatt, a member of one of Antigua's oldest families. What she has been to her husband in their long married life is best known to those who have had the pleasure of her intimidate acquaintance. Their golden wedding was celebrated in August 1894, when a public address, and a piece of gold plate were presented to the Doctor along with many presents for both from the people of Antigua.

In an appreciative sketch, it is only fair to mention the slight imperfections of one in whom there was so much good. The doctor had an explosive temper and a tongue which once started ran clear away. But it was like a mechanical toy, it could run only a certain distance; it could cause trouble occasionally, but the trouble was never serious as everyone recognized that the goodness of his heart exceeded the faults of his tongue. For the past ten years he had practically retired from practice and had taken up farming, of which he was always fond. He had owned or leased estates all over the island at different times, but as a planter and farmer he was certainly not successful. His plans and ideas were always too grand. Undoubtedly the worries caused by his financial losses accelerated his death.

For several years his professional income ranged between 2,000 pounds to 3,000 pounds per annum, except for the cost of educating his children, every penny earned by his own labour has been expended in Antigua. No doubt much of it was not wisely spent, for in his later years it was easy to lead him on the road he wished to walk, and a mere suggestion from a carpenter, or a mason, would next day produce a plan of a house.

Altogether, as a professional man, whose services were always at the call of the poor, as a public man, who almost alone has kept up the good name of Antigua, Dr Edwards for more than a quarter of a century stood head and shoulders over all - official or unofficial, European or Creole.

With no desire to be profane, and deploring the possibility of being judged so, we have often when one of the medical faculty has paid natures last debt, associated in our minds the utter impotence of man with the taunt addressed to the Worlds Redeemer, when, as man, he suffered and was powerless in the hands of his enemies - "he saved others, himself he cannot save ".

Over such a career, it would not be possible even remotely to conceive how many hundreds of his fellow creatures were relieved and even saved from death by his professional skill and attention. He could not himself but have been cognizant of symptoms of approaching dissolution - the sense that the pegs of the tabernacle were gradually losing hold, so that to him the sudden call could not have been a surprise. It did not certainly cause fear when in answer to the summons, he felt and expressed resignation the supreme fiat.

The large attendance of all classes at the Funeral Service at the Cathedral testified sufficiently to their respect for him. His body was interred at the family burial ground at All Saints which can now claim to hold all that there is of Antigua's 'Grand Old Man'. "

Arthur Elliot (Doctor Arthur Edwards - Born Jan 12th, 1853. and known as 'The young doctor'). Married Sarah Baynes. Died April 17th, 1897. **(Arthur Edwards and Sarah Baynes were my paternal great grandparents)** He was the younger son of Dr. William Henry Edwards and Georgianna Ledeatt. Born in Antigua - Jan. 12, 1853. Married - Sarah Baynes. Died in Antigua April 17th, 1897.

Dr. Arthur Elliot Edwards and Sarah Baynes

Samuel McDonald

My great grandfather John Scotland McDonald had a half brother, Samuel, who founded a vigorous branch of the family. His descendants are important contributors to Antiguan national life to this day.

Samuel was the son of Robert McDonald, who was born in Ireland in 1800 and worked as a merchant in Liverpool before seeking his fortune in Antigua sometime in the 1820s. There he prospered and had a son, Samuel, with an enslaved woman, Polly Roberts.

Samuel was born in 1827 and christened in St. John's Cathedral in 1929. He was supported by his father and worked as a young man in the business McDonald and Co. Thereafter he had a varied career. He was listed as a merchant in 1872, a baker in 1875, a notary in 1890, and an auctioneer at other times. In 1856, he married Amelia Mason. Their eldest son, Donald Edward (1858-1906), was a Methodist Minister; he married Ella Buckley, the daughter of the Rev. John Andrew Buckley, one of the first non-white Antiguans to become an ordained Moravian Minister. They went to British Guiana and lived there until the father died in 1906. Donald and Ella's ten children, who returned to Antigua with their mother, became key members of the new middle class then beginning to emerge.

I think of Samuel's slave mother, Polly Roberts, with a wonder that provokes me. What was her form of slavery and when was she freed? Was it before 1834 when slavery ended in Antigua? Or did Robert help her to freedom before then? Did she live to see her son a success in the community? She stays a nagging mystery in my mind—a mystery indeed as nearly every single human ever born is a mystery lost in all eternity.

Ian Donald Roy McDonald

The gold-coloured wooden fighter plane propeller from World War I hangs near the altar in St. George's Cathedral, St. John's, Antigua. The first time I saw it, I thought what a strange trophy to place in a house of peace and worship. But then I thought of the regimental flags which hang in Cathedrals around the world and remembered that there is not only a God of Peace and that men also worship bravery.

Propeller from Ian McDonald's plane shot down in
Mesopotamia - displayed in St. John's Cathedral Antigua

The propeller, belonging to a fighter plane he flew in battle, hangs, or used to hang, in the Cathedral in honour of my cousin, Flight Lieutenant Ian McDonald, my great-uncle Donald McDonald's son, who was an ace fighter plane pilot credited with twenty victims in the air in the Great War.

On one famous occasion he flew chivalrously alongside an enemy whose guns had fallen silent and at the point of a pistol

Kurt Wüsthoff's Biplane

aimed at close range forced him to land and give himself up as a prisoner of war. The prisoner in question was a celebrated German Air Ace, Kurt Wüsthoff, who was flying a Fokker Biplane.

During the dog fight with Ian's plane, a SE5, the German ran out of ammunition. The German's predicament was clear to Ian and was reinforced when the enemy pilot raised his hands in surrender. Ian pointed to where he wanted the German to land, in fact Ian's base. When the two planes were finally on the ground, the German was invited to a slap up dinner in Ian's mess. The next day this pilot was taken to a British prisoner of war camp. So Ian had made the first capture in the air of an enemy pilot.

Returning home to Antigua, he was given a tremendous hero's welcome in St. John's. Days of glory for the very young man – he had lied about his age to get into the Royal Flying Corps (as the Royal Air Force was called up to 1918). He tried to settle into normal life by beginning a career at the Antigua Sugar Factory. How could that work? Imagine the boredom of ordinary days in an apprentice's job in agriculture. Fame had touched him but perhaps more than that, the spur of danger, that addictive alteration in the brain which takes place when testing yourself against ultimate, lethal challenge.

Soon enough he reapplied to the RAF and resumed his military career. This time he was assigned to fight in Britain's colonial wars. And in a sortie during tribal warfare in Mesopotamia, he was shot down by ground fire. He crash-landed on a sandbank in the middle of the Euphrates. His fellow fliers signalled to him trying to indicate to which safe bank of the Euphrates he should swim. But he swam the wrong way. There he was captured and

Ian D.R. McDonald

was seen to be summarily executed. His body never came home. He was an only son.

I was named after him. I contemplate his life of bravery, sudden glory and early death. He never had time to settle into any pattern. The arc of my life has been completely different – very long, well administered, purposely uncombative except on the field of play, unlit by great drama, varied and successful but likely to vanish soon after being swallowed by the earth. It has been for me, and a few others, an excellent life. But for me no trophy will hang in a Cathedral. I sometimes wonder what he whose name I was given would have thought of me?

Dr. William Maclachlan McDonald

I remember my grandfather, Dr. William McDonald, OBE, as a slight, slim, upright man with a full head of snow-white hair cut nearly to a buzz. I remember on holiday in Antigua being with him and my father when they played golf on the Beach Hotel course near the sea at Hodges Bay. I remember them laughing and getting on well together with Grandpa McDonald swearing a bit more than my father at wayward shots. I liked being with them and they gave me a club to try some shots. My grandfather always seemed to me a serious, good man.

Dr. William Maclachlan McDonald standing on the front steps of Cliff House, Hodges Bay Antigua 1947

He was a colonial patriot. He interrupted his life to volunteer for service first in the Transvaal in the Boer War and then in World War I when he served in Egypt. But his life's mission was in medicine. He did important work in discovering hookworm in Antigua and promoting its treatment and his research and description of malaria also in Antigua was recognized and praised by the London School of Tropical Medicine. But his real, full-time career was as a dedicated GP. In Government and then in private practice he served the public for 50 years. That is long. He did not end up rich. Cliff House was his main possession. Long after he formally retired mothers brought their children to him at Cliff House where he maintained an informal surgery. Often there was no money but he saw the children anyway. Of course. I remember Grandma McDonald saying that some people brought eggs or vegetables or fruit to pay him.

An old Lebanese lady, in a lovely snatch of memory, told my sister Gillian that when she was a little girl visiting Dr. McDonald for a sore throat he asked her to put out her tongue and she was frightened he was going to do something terrible to it and she refused and refused even though her mother berated her. But the doctor was very calm and smiling. He quietly said to the mother "Don't worry at all, I know exactly what is wrong. This little girl hasn't got a tongue." At which, the old lady recalled, outraged she put out her tongue very far, showing him – there! She remembers that nearly 70 years before. I can see it.

One memory I have of the old doctor which I can date with absolute precision – 6th June, 1944. That day my father had gone out deep-sea fishing with some friends and took me along. We went far out beyond the reefs, beyond Prickly Pear Island, where the sea was deep blue. I love the memory of it – something I hadn't done before. The sea felt heavy under the boat. My father hooked two big fish and let me help him pull them in – barracudas, I remember them silver and dangerous as long swords unsheathed in the sun, long and gleaming, teeth razor sharp I was warned. Later, at night, grandpa McDonald came over to the small cottage,

Cliff House 1947

Edgewater, which my father and mother had rented for the holidays. He sat with my father and they talked animatedly about the momentous events in Europe that day, delighted and having drinks. I was bursting with my own great feat and wanted to tell my grandfather. My father finally let me interrupt and I told the story of the barracudas. Well, my grandfather was very pleased and he gave me a big salute and he told me I should remember that day for the rest of my life.

In the 1990s when I was visiting my sister Gillie and her husband Doug Howie in Antigua a taxi driver taking me to Cliff House from the airport told me when he was a little boy his mother brought him to see the old doctor at Cliff House. At the end of the trip the taxi-man got out the car and shook my hand

Archie McDonald, my father, at Edgewater, Antigua 1944

and thanked me because his mother had said the old doctor was a very good man. Something you remember and think about.

My grandfather, Dr. William McDonald, he lived such a full and useful life, he did so much unselfish good, he left his world so much better a place through his efforts – why is he not very well remembered? What can one say? We are watchmen on the shore. Waves receding are lost in the ocean always coming in.

Leo Seheult

I was six when my grandfather Leo Seheult died. I do not remember him except what I heard of him later. I regret very much I have no memory of being with him because it is clear he was a vivid and creative person. Judging from my own experience with my grandson Jacob age 3 onwards (he is now 6) there may well have been a good deal I learned from my grandfather Leo. This thought makes me want to live long enough so that Jacob does recall our being together and our many conversations. ("Granddad, are shadows real?" "What happened to yesterday?").

Leo Seheult's was born in Martinique. His grandfather was Jean Jacques Seheult, first French Vice-Consul in Trinidad, whom we have met. The Seheults had become a famous Trinidad family.

Leo Seheult

Leo was a brilliant young man from all accounts and he had a brilliant career as an engineer. In the public service of Trinidad and Tobago he did outstanding works. He has his quota of fame as the man who built the great bridge at St Joseph and, even more famously, the Treasury Building in Port-of-Spain, ultra-modern in its time. He was slated to become Trinidad's chief engineer in charge of all public works when he died at the age of 54. Cut off in his prime, people shook their heads.

When I was older I got to know the drastic repercussions on the family's fortunes of my grandfather Leo's premature death. The affluence bestowed by a good salary and, most importantly, by a full range of official perquisites – housing, servants, medical expenses, entertainment, horse and buggy and groom and then car and chauffeur – was overnight reduced to relative penury in the form of his widow's reduced pension and nothing more. Huge adjustments had to be made abruptly. My widowed grandmother, Emmie Seheult, boundlessly sweet-natured and kind as I remember her, had to go and share a house with her mother, a sister (Aunt Muriel, herself a widow) and great-aunt Anna. I know my parents, still a young couple at the time, chipped in financially and did so for the rest of the old peoples' lives.

Something all this showed was that often enough a public show of affluence was not based on personal wealth nor indeed did top public positions lead to the accumulation of private riches. Indeed one gets the impression that jobs in those times – certainly in my family – were done in the spirit of Marcus Aurelius in his Meditations: not expecting showy gratitude, far less enriching bribes, since that "would be like the eye demanding a reward for seeing."

As I got older I learned the story – whispered, hinted, explained. Leo Seheult was brilliant and dynamic but he gradually succumbed to alcoholism – at first enjoying drinks with the boys excessively and then becoming dependent. What happened was a great sadness, a tragedy really. In order to counteract the effects of hangover and get to work on time and clear-headed he begun to take injections (of what who can tell?) from a doctor (I never heard his name). All was well for quite a time. Presumably, however, to serve its purpose, what was being administered had to be increased and increased in strength. The result could have been foretold. He was 54 at the height of his powers when he died.

And then everything, as far as I can tell, was hushed up. I never asked why. It was dealt with as a family tragedy. I am not sure even now, after so many years, that I may be breaking family ranks by suggesting that there may have been an element a little darker than pure tragedy in my brilliant grandfather's death.

Donald McDonald

Donald McDonald

In my ancestry there is a poetry gene. It missed generations. It reappeared in me. I have a vague memory of a distant cousin telling me she had traced our heritage back to a 15th or 16th Century English poet, not one of the great ones but a poet all the same. And there was passionate Edward Dacres Baynes whose poetry and translations of Ovid, we have seen, have survived to be read after 200 years – and how many, after all, can make that claim?

Then there was my great-uncle Donald McDonald, father of the air force hero Ian McDonald. Donald McDonald was a businessman in Antigua but he wrote verse and he got around to publishing **Songs of an Islander** in London in 1917. When his only son was killed in battle so young the zest went out of him and he eventually committed suicide. The verse he wrote is full of patriotic fervor. So that his unquiet shade may know 100 years afterwards that his verse is read I quote from a poem, A Song of Content, about young men who died in England's wars. The terrible irony must have struck him to the heart a few years later when his own son died:

"All his boyish prospects ended, and their plans for life together –
With his death his mother's world has crumpled, life is spent,
But through all her grief she sees her boy a man with manhood's courage,
In the splendid message that he died content.

Tell the father who was waiting for his son to stand beside him,
And help him till his life on earth was spent,
He must finish now alone, strive to finish well alone,
For England's Honour he must live content."

Bronze Equestrian Statue of Queen Victoria - Prize awarded to John Scotland McDonald

Donald McDonald's (and my grandfather Dr. William Maclachlan McDonald's) father was John Scotland McDonald. He is another ancestor I would be glad to know much better. He was born in Antigua in 1938 and the public record shows that his main business of life was business – he took over the company McDonald & Co in 1865 – and bringing up a large family of 11 children. But when he was young, sent to study in London, he must have been a budding artist of some note since he won top prizes in two art competitions. What happened? There is no evidence that he developed his talent in later life. Who will ever know what dreams he set aside?

Issac Singer's sad reflection, "What the earth swallows is soon forgotten", about sums it up. And yet, that fleeting talent is not completely forgotten through the generations. Handed down to me, and now in our living room in full view at our home in BelAir Gardens in Guyana, there is a beautiful equestrian statue of the young Queen Victoria, one of 50 copies made at the time of the original work by the English sculpture Thomas Thornycroft dated 1853. It is the prize young John Scotland won in England for his art when he was a young man studying in London. I look at it and I think, as I often think how much has vanished we shall never know.

Hilda McDonald

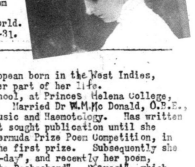

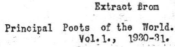

Extract from

Principal Poets of the World.
Vol. 1., 1930-31.

MC DONALD, Hilda (Mrs), is a European born in the West Indies, where she has lived for the greater part of her life. Educated at The Antigua Girls' School, at Princes Helena College, Ealing, England, and in Lausanne. Married Dr W.M.Mc Donald, O.B.E., of Antigua. Hobbies - Poetry, Music and Haemotology. Has written poetry for many years, but had not sought publication until she entered for The Poetry Review's Bermuda Prize Poem Competition, in which she was a joint winner of the first prize. Subsequently she sent a few poems to "Poetry of To-day", and recently her poem, "Quest", was a prize winner in "The Dechachord". "Quest", which has no rhyme, is distinctive, in that its form and rhythm make one forget the absence of rhyme. In this it differs from most modern poetry in which absence of rhyme is insistent.
    Address: Redcliffe House, Antigua, B.W.I.

M y grandmother, Hilda McDonald, née Edwards was a good poet. She might have made a name as one if she had found time to cultivate that demanding art and craft amidst the rest of her full and interesting life. She was a good wife tremendously helpful to her doctor husband in his profession and his research. She was a much loved mother of two sons and two daughters. And she had her own distinguished career – rising to be Chief Information Officer in the Antiguan colonial Government and becoming the first woman member of the

Antiguan Legislative Assembly. She corresponded with the famous editors of **BIM** in Barbados and **Kyk-Over-Al** in British Guiana – which, in a little tango step of fate, I was to edit many years later. And she wrote a few poems and published them in Sunflakes and Stardust (1956) which incorporated poems from a previous collection, which I cannot trace, entitled **Sea, Sun and Stardust**.

One afternoon when she was old and living in England she and I, on holiday from my job in British Guiana, sat in a Sussex garden alone having tea and cakes and talking principally about me and my plans. But I grew sad as she confided in me her feeling that she had indeed enjoyed a full and wonderful life but in her, nagging year after year and nothing done about it, lay heavy the regret that she had neglected a God-given talent. I denied quite insistently that she had done anything else but live a marvelously full and creative life. But she shook her head and made no answer and we talked of other things.

My grandmother wrote good clear poems. Here is an example that I think was unpublished –Hymn for the New Year (left).

> Hymn for the New Year 1960
>
> To whom I pray
> Lord, I have prayed,
> And beat my breast,
> Knowing my sins
> Too great to be confessed.
>
> Prayers all of self,
> All, all, of me,
> My sins, My sorrows,
> And mine infirmity.
>
> So great the noise
> Of what I say,
> I have forgot
> To whom I pray.
>
> Now, I am still:
> No more I pray,
> But let my thanks rise
> Night and day.
>
> Lord, grant me now,
> To hear – being still –
> That I may know,
> And do Thy Will.
>
> H. M. D.

There is one poem of hers in particular which I have always loved and I cannot read it without an ache coming in my eyes.

Evensong
(Yepton's Lagoon, Antigua)

Sunset had called in her colours,
But not yet was it dark,
The pool lay a mirror of silver,
 Without spot or mark.

When out from the green mirrored mangroves
Came a wonder of white,
A great heron wandering homewards,
Before it was night.

The moon and the reeds and the heron,
And the first white star,
Shone clear in the pool's bright mirror,
As I watched from afar.

The spell of that moment still holds me,
The mirror, the star, and the bird,
The beauty beyond all imagining,
The Silence where no whisper stirred.

And my heart sings aloud to its Maker,
In thanks and delight,
Who gave me that moment of Beauty,
Before it was night.

I pause to reflect. The more I have delved into family ancestry the more I have realized that there is nothing new under the sun. Many times in my life I have been told or read about some event or person and have thought "No, that is unbelievable, that could not have happened." But I come across a short account my grandmother, Hilda McDonald, has left of a conversation she had with her own grandmother in Antigua in January, 1915, and I am made aware that the ways and wonders of the world are infinitely strange and unpredictable wherever you slice history. Here is the conclusion of my grandmother's matter-of-fact account:

"In those days, Gran's father, Mr. Ledeatt lived at Tyrells and the Ottleys lived at Parrys. Miss Matilda Ottley was the Belle of Antigua. Gran's grandfather and grandmother but she cannot remember her grandfather Mr. Sedgwich, for he died when he was only 23 and just before Gran's mother was born.

Her Aunt, Mrs. Barbara Jervis Sedgwich married a Mr. Fitch who was superintendent of the Dockyard. This Mr. Fitch knew Nelson very well in the days when the ships used to lie in the Dockyard for the hurricane months. Her husband died after they had only been married a few years and she got a pension from the naval authorities and went to live with Gran's father and mother. She was very eccentric and always wore her hair cut short and did not wear a cap which Gran said was a great offense to her mother. There was a Mrs. Allman, wife of one of the officers at the Blockhouse who often used to stay at Tyrells with Grans' people.

Darron Wilkinson was the rector in Falmouth, then he was chaplain to the forces and used to entertain the officers a great deal. It was at a dinner party at his house that Gran was taken into dinner by the famous Dr. Barry who was an army doctor, and after his death, it was found out that he was a woman. Gran says he was a small delicate looking man and there was always some mystery about him for he enjoyed privileges which none of the other officers enjoyed and he lived in a little house all alone at the foot of Monks Hill. It was thought that he was a scion of Royalty as he was so very privileged. After he left Antigua he did the most outrageous things and did not get punished for them. In South Africa, he slapped a fellow officer in the face, and laid a horsewhip across the shoulders of another officer. Gran says she knew him well as he often used to ride up to Tyrells to see them. He was a vegetarian and took no wine. Old Dr. Odlum lived at Clarence House and Gran says he must have been in on the secret, for this Dr. Barry was very ill once and he was moved to Clarence House where Dr. Odlum attended him.

The sundial at the Dockyard marks the place where Lord Camelford shot Lieut Peterson. They wished to go to a dance in St. Johns and only one could leave the ships. Lord Camelford ordered Lieut Peterson to remain on Board and he refused and Lord Camelford promptly shot him dead."

• • • • •

Sundial at Nelson's Dockyard in Antigua

About the time the 19th century was turning into the 20th the family was prominent in Antigua – in colonial administration and politics, in business, in the ownership of property, in the professions, in social and cultural life. By the time I was a boy and growing up in the late 1940s that was no longer so. After one time is another. The moving finger writes. The name was still well-known and Cliff House in Hodges Bay located in incomparable, wind-swept beauty remained but the family had retreated from influence, retired, dispersed.

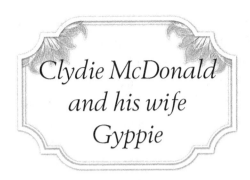

Clydie McDonald and his wife Gyppie

Clydie McDonald and his wife Gyppie 1940
Photo courtesy Agnes Meeker

Uncle Clydie and Aunt Gyppie were reminders of past glory – landed gentry in miniature you could say. Uncle Clydie was a younger brother of my grandfather Dr. William McDonald. He and his wife lived in High Point an old distinguished sugar plantation house on a hill in the middle of the American base near Hodges Bay. On holiday in the 1940s I visited them a few times. I remember them, wonderful old people with a special stubborn pride and courtesy of manner and patience which struck me. And an impression of dusty beautiful old furniture and rugs not suited to the tropics and one big painting of Roman ruins on one wall I remember. But the main thing was Uncle Clydie was blind and Aunt Gyppie was deaf. ("She sees for me, I hear for her"). They got along well like that, Uncle Clydie seemed to know every inch of High Point never feeling around, more importantly they knew every inch of each other's soul. What more did they need by then? It seemed a run-down place but beautiful and my heart went out to them.

High Point was the name of a small sugarcane estate which once had its own little sugar making factory complete with brick chimney. The estate, located in an area of the island which was particularly dry, never made much money at the best of times. I remember someone saying: "Clydie and Gyppie never had enough money to visit England!"

When the war came one of the bases which Britain made available to America in the "destroyers for bases" deal was in Antigua and the Americans identified the area around High Point as the place they wanted to locate their air-base. They were very good about allowing Uncle Clydie and Aunt Gyppie to continue living at High Point for the rest of their lives – so there the old house was on a hill in the middle of the base. The old people were not troubled.

They were also compensated for the small estate – land worth a fortune today. I never heard the amount of the compensation. Indeed I heard the money was never located – the rumour being that payment was made to some bank in America and that no record was ever found of this when the old people's affairs were being sorted out. I cannot understand this because I would have thought a request to the American authorities would have solved the problem.

High Point – 1940s
Photo courtesy Agnes Meeker

Well, it all may have been sorted out. The way I think of it – at the end Uncle Clydie Aunt Gyppie had themselves, what did they want money for? But, then, I wasn't a direct descendant.

Emily Seheult née Gray

As I, whatever the I in me is, examines the infinity of memories stored in my mind, the saddest I become is thinking how little of note I remember of my grandmother Emmie Seheult. After all, for many years in my schooldays at Queens Royal College in Port-of-Spain I stayed in her modest home at 84 Dundonald Street during the week in term time. After her glory days as wife of civil service royalty she seemed to bear no grudge against the unkindness of life. She was so sweetly natured.

Emily Seheult

And I have nothing but a sense of being loved by her very much and looked after, her eldest grandchild, cared for almost hand and foot. I have the sweetest, good memory of being loved by her and an abiding sense of her anxious concern for my welfare and success. I remember also she was the peacemaker in the house – great-aunt Anna and Aunt Muriel did not get on and my grandmother was constantly pacifying ruffled feathers.

And it wasn't that she was distant – she hugged me tight all her days. I know there was sadness in her life – the premature and tragic death of her husband, Grandpa Leo, and also years ago the death of a son at birth. Yet she remained a happy person. I think she was one of those people whose nature is most valiant and who through their concern never to make things worse always refuse to inflict their own pain and troubles and doubts on others.

I have these general very good and loving impressions. But I have no specific memories of talks with her or outings or stories or jokes she told to me or warnings or advice or praise or prayers like my great-aunt Anna in her rocking chair. There is a blur of love. It does not come into focus.

My grandmother, Emmie Seheult, died when I was in England at Cambridge. She died of cancer. Some years later talking about her I was told to the end she tried not to be too much trouble.

Yet there is one specific remembrance I do have of my grandmother who so loved me. The day I left for England to go up to University she gave me her golden wedding ring. I found a finger where it would fit securely – the little finger on my left hand. It is a heavy gold ring with one word inscribed on the inside of the band – Leo. The gold ring is 106 years old. I have worn it on that same finger for 66 years. I am looking at it now. I twist it round and round as I often do.

Leo's ring

Uncle Bertie Harragin

Lieut.Col Harragin

I have a memory of meeting my Uncle Bertie – A.E. "Bertie" Harragin, my mother's uncle, great Aunt Clementine Collin's only son. He died in 1941 when I was eight years old so it can't have been long before he died that we met. I remember a tall, elegant even graceful figure who did not condescend but had serious, interesting things to say. I wish I could remember what those things were but I know they were not pat-on-the-head stuff. When I was older my father told me that he had been asked by Uncle Bertie if I was a speed or endurance runner – because that would be important to know in any future sporting career I might have. I wish he had lived longer.

"What the earth swallows is soon forgotten." In his era Uncle Bertie was the greatest all-round sportsman by far in Trinidad. Lieutenant-Colonel Harragin was also a distinguished soldier and fought with extreme gallantry and dedication in Palestine in World War I. At the battle of Damieh on the Jordan he was awarded the D.S.O for his leadership and bravery and earned the special praise of the Commander in Chief General Allenby.

Subsequently he had a fine career in the Police Force in Trinidad and rose to be Deputy Inspector General – much admired in his profession.

But his fame was truly in the field of sports. He was an outstanding athlete. At one time he held the West Indian record in the 100 and 220 sprints, the 120 hurdles, the shot put, the pole vault and for throwing the cricket ball and the Trinidad record for the 440 and 880. It intrigues me that his record of throwing the cricket ball 128 yards 4 inches may be the longest such throw ever officially recorded since around that time throwing the cricket ball stopped being an event in competitions.

He was a leading footballer. He was a champion amateur jockey. He was an outstanding oarsman. He was one of Trinidad's best cyclists. I wonder what else he excelled at? It seems unreal.

Yet all these exploits are not what bestowed on him the greatest fame. Because cricket was by far the most popular sport in Trinidad and indeed the West Indies, the ordinary man's obsession, it was Uncle Bertie's extraordinary prowess as a cricketer and Captain of the national team which made him universally celebrated. In that role it is not too much to say that he became a legend. He first played for Trinidad in 1898, captained for the first time in 1901 and thereafter was a dominating figure in inter-colonial play until he retired in 1921. Only to be induced to come out of retirement in 1932 to lead Trinidad against perennial rival, and recently unbeatable, Barbados. Uncle Bertie was 55. He led Trinidad to victory. I like to think of it.

In 1906 he toured with the West Indies team in England as Vice-Captain. In the first match of the tour the West Indies played W.G. Grace's XI. Uncle Bertie – I have seen the report –

hit the Grand Old Man of cricket for six sixes in a swashbuckling innings of 50. I like to think of that too.

How can one measure the full nature of any man? When Bertie Harragin died it was said he was by far the most popular sportsman ever produced in Trinidad. It was said of him that he epitomized honesty, grace, charm, strength of character mixed with modesty and sympathy for others that never failed him. Fine words indeed but even finer for me is what C.L.R. James wrote – C.L.R. James, the great West Indian historian and intellectual, author of **Beyond A Boundary**, the best book ever written about cricket:

> *"Old Constantine was an independent spirit. Cricket must have meant a great deal to him. Yet when some dispute broke out with the authorities he refused to play anymore. One who saw it told me how A.E. Harragin left the Queen's Park pavilion, walked over to where Constantine was sitting in the stands and persuaded him to come back. Few people in Trinidad, white or black, could refuse Bertie Harragin anything. He was an all-round athlete of rare powers, of singular honesty and charm. I would have accepted any cricket pronouncement of his at face value. He was one of the very few white men in the island at the time who never seemed aware of the colour of the person he was speaking to."*

And writing of the emergence of young Learie Constantine CLR had this to say:

> *"Even to my interested eye he was full of promise, but not more. Major Harragin, however, was captaining Trinidad in the evening of his cricketing days. He knew a cricketer when he saw one and he probably could see much of the father in the son. Practically on his own individual judgment he put Learie in the intercolonial tournament of 1932. But for the Major's sharp eye and authority it is most unlikely that he would have got in so early."*

Just to think that a little of Uncle Bertie's bloodline may have leaked into mine makes me feel better than I am.

Sir Arthur William Baynes McDonald

When he was 86 or so Uncle Arthur learned I was in England on vacation from my job in Guyana and sent a message inviting me to crew with him in a yachting race in which he was competing. I replied that I was too old and unfit to accept. He got someone else and nearly won the race.

My father's older brother – in his pomp Air Marshal Sir Arthur McDonald of the Air Council of the Royal Air Force. He was a life-force, one of the most charismatic men I have met. Charismatic but not intimidating. When I first went to England at the age of 18, to go up to Cambridge, he was a VIP but didn't show it at all. His kind eyes and his chuckling laugh and his smile were like my father's and that helped. He put me at my ease – conversation that drew me out and gave me confidence. Thereafter he helped me whenever he could while I was at University.

If there is someone of lasting fame in the family it is Uncle Arthur. He rose and rose to be Air Marshal helping to run the RAF at the very top. He had done experimental work of great distinction with fighter planes. At one point in an illustrious career he was seconded to be first Commander of the Pakistan Air Force. But more importantly in the greater scheme of things, he was in earlier days in the forefront of the team which tested super-secret radar in the 1930s and brought it to success in time to be decisive in winning the Battle of Britain. The Air Minister at the time told him and the small team testing the application of the new technology that an Empire's fate depended on them. I have seen a letter he wrote my father in which he describes the excitement when blips appeared on the experimental monitor indicating airliners rising out of Schiphol international airport hundreds of miles away and they knew for the first time that the device worked and early warning in battle would be possible.

In the sidelines of his outstanding Air Force career he was a famous yachtsman, no doubt learning the rudiments of that sport sailing in the blue and sunlit seas off the windy coasts of Antigua in his boyhood. In 1948 at the Olympic Games in England he captained the British yachting team and took the Olympic oath on behalf of all the sportsmen.

A Great Man, no doubt. To me he was an astonishing presence but mainly a good and helpful and friendly uncle.

Arthur McDonald on his boat, the Firefly, at the 1948 Olympic Games, also called the Austerity Games. Photo by Life Magazine photographer.

Arthur taking the Olympic Oath in front of the semi-circle of flagbearers of the competing nations at the 1948 Olympics.

Archie McDonald And Thelma Seheult

Archie McDonald

Thelma Seheult

In my rich inheritance there my parents are – my beloved father, John Archie McDonald and his bride Thellie, Thelma Camilla Seheult, my beloved mother. I do not see how there could be better parents than they were – generous, kind, understanding but firm in correcting faults and misconceptions about how to behave in respect of oneself and towards others, not too solemnly adult, loving above all. Perhaps too good because they made the path of childhood and the course of youth so good, so untrammelled, that the raw challenges of grown-up life came as unexpected shocks. When, for instance, my first marriage went wrong it was a shocking revelation of what could happen which I never had reason to conceive.

No. 1 Carmody Road 1962

They were the best of parents in instilling in their children so that it was unshakeable a sense of self-worth and personal dignity and the need to respect others and do good in the world. Their love was unconditional and so too in return was their children's love for them.

In what we inherit, so much depends on the parents. Their daily, persevering, unending love and interest and example taught lessons which reached deep into us; we were nurtured and our minds and souls were formed into shapes and disciplines that have lasted all our lives. I am in my 85th year and the work and love my father and mother devoted to their children, of whom I was the first-born, remain in my memory to this day. I recall vividly the distinction and the joy of my days as their son. They lived the standards we learned to expect of ourselves. Deep respect was owed to people. Ram the gardener, drunk and erratic sometimes but he was treated kindly and was an important human being in the family. We saw that the good in people must be found out and brought forward for inspection and for praise.

At six years old I am in agony and very frightened. In hospital an infected appendix is removed. The night comes when no visitors are allowed. My mother says they with their strongest arms will have to carry her out screaming if they think she will not stay and I still remember her gentleness and lullabies all that long night and all the other nights. "Golden slumber kiss your eyes." Quite recently I wrote a poem about this vivid memory.

My Mother Sings Me Lullabies

pain seized me I cried out in horror
eighty years gone his gold watch is still swinging
rotund Dr. Littlepage whispers I will die
unless I get to hospital he will call the surgeon
woke from blackness after they had stifled me
white-coated torturers tore me from my parents
the cracked ice shone like diamond chips
silver spoon my mother placed against my lips
tears glistened in her eyes like diamonds too I saw
she brought mercy to me in my raging thirst
I cried and cried for her she never left my side
no visitors at night her anger struck them down
"you tie me up with ropes I will still come in"
beloved mother such fierce beauty I have never known
I knew then all my life I would be safe forever

I could not make head nor tail of calculus. Numbers have never lined up easily in my brain. But my father's patient hours of tuition, with hugs of encouragement in between, helped see me through to a maths distinction in the School Certificate.

It is nearly 70 years ago. I am returning with my father from playing my first competitive tennis matches, and my mother, who could never bear to come to watch, always greets me with her shining smile and a hug of utmost love. I was a lord of the universe, win or lose. Confidence grows. The world cannot undo you.

When I was about fifteen and listed my ambitions – which included as a start winning the Island scholarship, winning the national tennis title and going on to win Wimbledon – my father approved. But he pointed out that another list came first: the work and disciplines I had to pursue if I hoped to make these dreams become reality.

Once I petulantly smashed my racket on the court in a game and to this day I feel the steady, grey eyes of my father lock on mine afterwards, and I hear his quiet words: "My son, if you have to behave like that, I do not believe you should play this game."

My father was 89 years old when he died, his long life spanning nearly the whole of the 20th century. It was a century of change never before equaled in history, miracles of human achievement, depths of human evil. Throughout this turbulence my father never lost his bearings. His compass was always pointed in the direction of truth, fortitude, concern for others. In my own life I have met many remarkable people, some of high rank in the top echelons of the world. I can truly say I have never met anyone whose judgments were more often right than my father's, whose understanding of what is good and bad in man has been more accurate, whose conclusions about what really matters in life have been so true.

Not long before my father died I visited him and my mother at Cliff House. Long after I wrote a poem about my memory of the visit.

Father

he weakened in his final days
"too tired to listen to the radio
too tired" he smiled "to stay alive"
he rubbed his grey and stubbled face
said sorry that he couldn't shave
he who kept himself so well

I sit close and grasp his mottled hand
the liver spots have multiplied
my sadness makes it hard to breathe
calm grey eyes once steadied me
young and lithe on court and field
taught me so much I came to love
his love and confidence in me
meant nothing really could go wrong
way way back suddenly I see him
stride toward me with a bound of joy
takes and lifts me to the heavens high
soaring laughing – again! again! –
puts me down and hugs me hard
oh how I loved him then forever
forever my heart could burst
he asks me how I'm doing now
his free hand takes out a handkerchief
dabs the lids "not tears you know
just an old man's rheumy eyes"
wants me so bad to smile with him
"you have always made me proud"
the wind blows off the green-blue sea
as he has known for thirty years
"son get me up" I half-carry him
to look down on the beloved sea
where years ago we swam and sported
he leaned on me we watched together
where far far far far out the green and blue
fades to grey and then to nothingness

Afterthought

Nothingness. Inheritance sets out to rescue a little from what is the fate of most individual and family histories.

So much vanishes in even one generation and nearly everything except a few dates and dry statistics and faded pictures in old albums in the generations before that. I don't know if it will be different in a digital age with millions of pictures and billions of words incessantly recorded in the social media. The greater challenge then may be not to find what is left but to select from what remains forever. How a book like this will be composed 50 years from now with everything floating eternally in the cloud I have no idea. Perhaps no one will need or want to write such a book. But if such books are still written then they will have one thing in common with this one. They will be labours of pride and love.

Inheritance derives overwhelmingly from love of parents and family and a feeling of how much we owe to the long line of those who generation after generation worked and loved and laughed and cried and whose endeavours through the years built our substance and finally breathed life into us.

My sister Robin has been the prime mover in this book. She has been the family archivist and chief instigator in finding things. She has been the main gatherer and compiler. The two of us discussed concept and framework and many ideas as the work

Robin, Ian, Gillian, Heather, Archie, Archie jr., Thelma and Monica at No. 1 Carmody Road, St. Augustine, Trinidad on the occasion of Heather's wedding to Liam Murray on 16th June, 1957

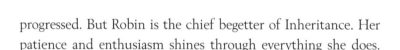

progressed. But Robin is the chief begetter of Inheritance. Her patience and enthusiasm shines through everything she does. Inheritance would not have been done without her.

Our sisters Heather Murray, Gillian Howie and Monica Purkis and our brother Archie have been keen and loving supporters and contributors. We live far apart – Robin in Canada, Heather in Scotland, Gillian in Antigua, Monica and Archie in England, myself in Guyana – but the family bond is strong, a goodly inheritance in its own right. May the generations which spring from us be as fortunate.

The English novelist L.P. Hartley wrote: "The past is a foreign country: they do things differently there." Yes, I see what he means – look at those old photographs: the fashions, the number of hats, the strange ancient-looking cars in the background, the elegant wooden buildings, no one using a smartphone! But, no, he is fundamentally wrong – delve a little deeper, get to know the people a little more, what they did and tried to do, their dreams and desires and hurts and joys, how they lived and loved and worked and fought and played and died, their triumphs and tragedies: that is no foreign country of the heart and soul – that is home to all of us. What one inherits, and what one in turn passes on, is the stuff of life itself and always will be.

IAN A. MCDONALD
Born: April 18, 1933 – 'Bessie's House' Carmody Rd., St. Augustine Trinidad WI

Father
John Archibald McDonald
B. July 25th, 1906, St. Kitts, W.I.
Married – Thelma Camilla Seheult
At St. Joseph Church, St. Joseph, Trinidad
July 9th, 1932
Agricultural Dept, Trinidad 1928-29
Cacao Research Chemist & Lecturer in Physics
Physics & Meteorology ICTA, Trinidad 1930-36
Planting Attorney, Gordon Grant & Co.Ltd.1936-1966
Retired 1966 – moved to Cliff House, Antigua May 1, 1973
D. Aug. 6th, 1995 Cliff House, Antigua

Mother
Thelma Camilla Seheult
B. August 31st, 1912, Tacarigua, Trinidad
Married. – John Archibald McDonald
At St. Joseph Church, St. Joseph, Trinidad
July 9th, 1932 – 2 sons, 4 daughters,
All born in Trinidad
Home: 1 Carmody Road, St. Augustine, Trinidad
Moved to Cliff House, Antigua May 1st, 1973
D. Mar. 7th 1998 Cliff House, Antigua

WEST INDIES

Son of
Dr. William M. McDonald & Hilda Edwards
Medical Practitioner-Leeward Islands,Antigua
Antigua & Barbuda, St. Kitts & Nevis 1896-1951
B. April 16th, 1870, St. Johns, Antigua, W.I.
Married – Hilda Ellen Maud Edwards Aug.26, 1902
St. Mary's Collegiate Chapel, Port Elizabeth, South Africa
(Service with R.A.M.C. in Boer War
Active Medical Research on Ancylostomiasis (Hook Worm)
And Malaria in Antigua (Reports in British Medical Journal)
1951 Cliff House, Antigua

Daughter of
Leo Gabriel Seheult & Emily Gray
B. Nov.12, 1885 Fort de France, Martinique
Lived at Santa Aqua Estate, Arima,Trinidad
Married – Emily Clarita Gray 1911 Trinidad
Civil Eng. Trinidad Public Works Dept.1909-1939
Executive Director P.W.D. 1932-1939
D. Trinidad, 1939
(Leo's wife Emily died in Trinidad Jan.1956
(Emily was daughter of Norah Collins and William
Gray – son of Alexander Robert Gray
B. in Lanarkshire, Scotland
M. Emily Francis Webster)

Son of
John Scotland McDonald M. Katherine Dora Maclachlan

(See page 2)

Son of
Louis Adhemar Seheult. M. Louise de Maury de Lapeyrouse

(See page 3)

IAN A. MCDONALD

My great grand father and great grand mother on my father's side were:

John Scotland McDonald   *Married*   **Katherine Maclachlan**

B. 1838 in Antigua W.I.
M. 1860 in Port Glasgow, Scotland
Merchant, Managing Director of
McDonalds & Co. St. Johns, Antigua 1865-1900
D. Dec, 18th, 1902 in Nursing Home in London
Buried in Norwood Cemetery

B. Apr.12th, 1844 in Kilmacolm Parish of Glasgow
D. Apr.19th, 1917 at Grays Hill, Antigua

Son of   *Daughter of*

Robert McDonald   *Married*   **Jane Elizabeth Miller**   **Rev. William Maclachlan**

B. 1800 in Lechpatrick,
Co.Tyrone Northern Ireland
Emigrated to Antigua 1820s
Founded the Firm of McDonald & Co.
General Merchants and Shipping Agents

daughter of
Capt. Miller T.R.N
was captain of the
'Theseus' and fought at
the Battle of Guadaloupe
In Nelson's Navy
& mentioned in dispatches

Feb.18, 1795, Kilbrandon Argyleshire
Lived in Reformed Presbyterian House
Kilmacolm Parish of Glasgow
M. 1836 to Margaret McDonald

Grandfather of Robert McDonald
Took part in the Battle of Culloden
April 27th, 1746. After that disastrous
defeat, Clanranald McDonalds fled to
Northern Ireland to escape the genocidal
Ravages of the Duke of Cumberlands troops

Son of

Archibald Maclachlan
Kilbrandon Argyleshire about 1765
(Records of Maclachlan in Parochial
Registers of Kilbrandon and Kilmacolm)

(SCOTLAND)

Clanranald McDonalds originated from
N.W. Scotland and the Western Isles
Which was their ancestreal home centered
On Castle Tioran on a Tidal Islet In Loch Moidart
Built in 1353 by the first wife of John Isla
Where it still stands today.

IAN A. MCDONALD

My great grandfather and great grand mother on my mother's side were:

Louis Adhemar Seheult	*Married*	**Louise de Maury de Lapeyrouse**

Louis Adhemar Seheult
B. Aug. 16th, 1855 Trinidad, W.I
('ADhemar's father Jean Jacques had secured a
French education provided for by the French
Govt. Adhemar was 12 years old when he and his
Brothers were sent to France. At some point he
Attended L'Ecole Nationale Superiere des Mines
De Paris where he got his degree in Engineering
Adhemar spent a lot of his time in Martinique
Where he had a business L.Seheult &Cie
In St.Pierre and also had a significant stake in a
Sugar estate in Ste. Luce, Martinique.
After a brief illness, Adhemar died Jan.31st, 1916 at
The home of his nephew and son-in-law
Fernand J. Seheult at Verdant Vale Estate, Arima, Trinidad

Louise de Maury de Lapeyrouse
B.?
D. Oct. 19th, 1892 Aqua Santa Estate
Guanapo, Arima, Trinidad

Daughter of:
Louis de Maury de Lapeyrouse
Son of:
Louis de Maury de Lapeyrouse
Son of:
Louis Michel de Maury de Lapeyrouse

Son of *(FRANCE)*

Jean Jacques Alexandre Seheult
B. 14th April 1794 Nantes, France.
Arrived Martinique 1820s was First French Consul Trinidad
1839-1865
M. Anne Joseph Cecile Losea De Verteuil (1809-1881) on Jun 3rd, 1837
At the church of the Mission of Santa Rosa de Arima, Trinidad
D. Mar.20, 1865 Martinique

Son of

Jacques Alexis de Verteuil – Note: Jacques Alexis de Verteul and Louis Michel de Maury de Lapeyrouse were among
The French Aristocrat families who fled from the terror of the French Revolution at the end of the 18th Century and
came to reside in various islands of the West Indies, including Trinidad.

IAN A. MCDONALD

My grandmother on my father's side was –

Hilda Ellen Maud Edwards *(see page 1)*
B. Aug. 3rd, 1883 in Antigua, West Indies
M. Dr. William Maclachlan McDonald
On Aug. 26th, 1902 at St. Mary's Collegiate Church
Port Elizabeth, South Africa.
Gave a lifetime of service to Antigua as a member
Of the City Commissioners of St. Johns,

(ANTIGUA)

Member of the Antigua Legislative Council
British Representative in Antigua.
During World War II she was Government
Information Officer in charge of Radio Antigua Reuter's
Correspondant and Correspondant for West Indian
Committee Circular.
Her poems were published in booklet form called
'Sunflakes and Stardust' by thre Poetry Guild of England.

Daughter of

Dr, Arthur Elliot Edwards	*Married*	**Sarah Baynes**
B. Jan.12th, 1855 in Antigua		1860 – 1836 Antigua
Medical Practitioner		
D. April 1st, 1897, in Antigua		*Daughter of*

Son of

Edwin Donald George Vincent Baynes
1828-1884
Dr. William Henry Edwards
Colonial Secretary Leeward Islands
B. Aug.1st, 1817 at Frogmore S. Devon England
and sometime Governor of Tobago
Emigrated to Antigua July 1842
Medical Practitioner Antigua 1842-1899
Died June 4th, 1899 - Buried at All Saints, Antigua

Son of

Edward Dacres Baynes
B. 1795
Lt. Royal Aretillery 1811
President of Council of Monserrat
D. Nov.5th 1863 in Antigua

IAN A. MCDONALD
My great, great, great Grandfdather on my father's side was (see Page 4)

Edward Dacres Baynes
B. 1795
D. Nov. 5th, 1863 in Antigua
Lieutenant Royal Artillery. He
He met Francesca di San Guiliano
in Sicily and persuaded her to marry and
and elope with him.
He entered the Colonial Service in 1833
Jamaica 1833 – 1840. Montserrat 1841-1856
Antigua 1856-1863

Married 1818

Francesca di San Guiliano
B. 1800 in Catania Sicily
D. Dec. 28th, 1863 in Antigua
She was the granddaughter of
Marchese de San Guiliano
She was a novitiate at a convent
and ran away with Lieut. Baynes
to spend the rest of her life in
the West Indies.

Son of

Thomas Baynes
Born on 1792. Died 1818
Captain Royal Navy

(EUROPE & MEDITERRANEAN)

<u>Note:</u>   Records of Baynes Family have been obtained from
British Army & Navy records & from British Colonial Office
Records and Old Family Papers..

Son Of

Sir Arthur Baynes
B. 1722. Died in Southhampton
England- June 25th, 1789. Medical Doctor.
Joined Royal Navy June 5th, 1756
Transferred to Army and appointed
Surgeon Commander of Gibraltar Garrison Jan. 18, 1757
Until his death in 1789

Married 1756

Judith Lambert
Born 1936 – Died May 30th, 1770 (Tragic accident)
Note: Judith Lambert was the daughter of
Sir John Lambert who was a banner resident
in Paris at the time of the marriage of the
Dauphin of France (afterward King Louis XVI to
Marie Antoinette of Austria. Sir John Lambert invited
His daughter Judith Baynes (Lambert) and her husband
To stay in Paris to witness the Royal Wedding.
Judith age 34 was killed in a fireworks explosion
during the festivities.

IAN A. MCDONALD

My great great grandfather on my father's side was (see page 4)

Dr. William Henry Edwards
B. Aug. 1, 1817 Frogmore, South Devon
England, Emigrated to Antigua Jul.1842
Medical Practitioner in Antigua 1842-1899
D. June 4th, 1899 in Antigua
Buried at All Saints, Antigua

Married

Georgiana Ledeatt
B. Mar. 21st, 1823 in Antigua
M. Aug.1, 1844 to
Dr. W. H. Edwards
D. June 25th, 1918.
Buried at All Saints, Antigua

Son of

John Wakeham Edwards
Born 1793.
D. Aug. 3, 1854.
Buried at Southpool

Married

Daughter of

Catherine Spry
B. Jul. 7th 1797
Stoke Dameral, Devon
M. 1815
D. Dec, 1st 1817

Note: Ledeatt family came out to Antigua Among the first English Settlers about 1668, together with such well know families as the Codringtons, Willoughbys, and Nugents.
(Reference :- History of Antigua by Vere Oliver)

Son of

Roger Edwards
B. Mar.15, 1762
D. Sep. 2nd 1825

William Spry
Naval Lieutenant on H.M.S. Formidable
which took part in the naval Battle of the Saints
On April 12th, 1782

Son of

Caleb Edwards of High House
B. 1718 at High House,
East Portlemouth, Devon
D. Sep. 15th 1790

Note: High House Portlemouth is still Preserved today and occupied. It is under the care of the Ministry of Works as a typical 17th Century Yeomans Farmer's Cottage.

(DEVONSHIRE, ENGLAND)

Note: Records of Edwards family (yeoman farmers) have been extracted from Parish Registers at Portlemouth Stokenham, Frogmore, Kingsbridge, Chivelstone, Exeter, going back to Walter Edwards of Middlecoombe Died March 18th, 1570.

CPSIA information can be obtained
at www.ICGtesting.com
Printed in the USA
LVHW091129181120
671982LV00001B/38